Pirates

Philip Steele

KINGFISHER
NEW YORK

KINGFISHER
LONDON & NEW YORK

Distributed in the U.S. and Canada by Macmillan,
175 Fifth Ave., New York, NY 10010

Library of Congress Cataloging-in-Publication Data

Steele, Phillip W.
 Pirates / Phillip Steele.
    p. cm. -- (Kingfisher readers level 4)
 1. Pirates--Juvenile literature. I. Title.
 G535.S742 2012
 910.4'5--dc23

                            2012036289

Series editor: Thea Feldman
Literacy consultant: Ellie Costa, Bank Street College, New York
Text for U.S. edition written by Thea Feldman

ISBN: 978-0-7534-6764-0 (HB)
ISBN: 978-0-7534-6765-7 (PB)

Kingfisher books are available for special promotions
and premiums. For details contact: Special Markets
Department, Macmillan, 175 Fifth Ave.,
New York, NY 10010.

For more information, please visit
www.kingfisherbooks.com

Printed in China
9 8 7 6 5 4 3 2
2TR/1012/WKT/UNTD/105MA

Contents

Pirate attack!

Imagine you are a sailor living about 300 years ago. You have been at sea for many weeks, and you haven't seen another ship in all that time. Suddenly a sail appears on the horizon. Does it belong to a friend or an enemy? As the ship gets nearer, you realize it is full of pirates!

Pirates are people who attack ships at sea. They may steal money or jewelry. They may carry off valuable **cargo** or take over the whole ship! Pirates may take people hostage or even kill them. There have been pirates in almost every part of the world for as long as people have sailed in boats. And there are still pirates on the attack today.

Pirate speak

Pirates and sailors living 300 years ago had their own special way of talking. They called the sea bottom, with all its sunken ships, "Davy Jones's locker."

Pirates fought with deadly weapons when they attacked a ship.

Who became pirates?

People became pirates for all sorts of reasons. Some, like many **buccaneers**, were violent criminals who had escaped from jail. The buccaneers settled on the Caribbean islands in the 1600s.

Bartholomew Roberts was a Welsh pirate who stole a lot of money.

Roche Brasiliano

The cruelest buccaneer of all was a Dutchman named Roche Brasiliano. He roasted his Spanish enemies alive!

Some pirates started out as **mutineers**. These were sailors who rebelled against their captain. A Scottish sailor named John Gow led a **mutiny** in 1724. He murdered his ship's officers and became a pirate. Gow was soon feared by sailors from Spain to Scotland.

Some pirates started as very poor people who just wanted to get rich. Before they sailed, pirate crews agreed on how to share any treasure they stole. They also agreed to pay crew members if they were wounded in the fighting.

Pirates or privateers?

When was a pirate not a pirate?
When he was a **privateer**!
Kings, queens, or governments
often gave sea captains, called
privateers, special permission to
attack ships that belonged to
enemies of their country.

In 1523, a French captain named
Jean Fleury captured two Spanish
ships as they sailed home from the
Caribbean. Jean carried off piles of gold,
but he claimed that he was a privateer, not
a pirate. He had papers to prove it.

A big bang!

Henry Morgan was a Welsh buccaneer and
privateer. In 1669, his crew blew up their
own ship by mistake, killing 250 people
on board.

Jean Fleury and his crew attacked Spanish treasure ships.

Seafarers were often seen as heroes in their own country but as pirates in another. Between 1577 and 1580, an English sea captain named Francis Drake sailed around the world. On the way, he attacked Spanish ships. When he came home, he was **knighted** by Queen Elizabeth I. The people of Spain were furious.

Women pirates

Most sailors thought it was unlucky to have any women on board a ship at sea. Even so, some women did fight on pirate ships, often more fiercely than the men.

Grace O'Malley lived on the west coast of Ireland in the 1560s. She and her crews attacked ships up and down the coast. When the English complained about her piracy, she sailed to London and demanded to meet Queen Elizabeth I face to face! It turned out they respected each other.

Mary Read was
an English pirate
who sailed to the
Caribbean in 1719.
Her ship was captured by another pirate
named John Rackham, or "Calico Jack." Mary
happily joined his crew, which included Jack's
girlfriend, Anne Bonny. Mary and Anne
both fought fiercely, using
axes and swords.

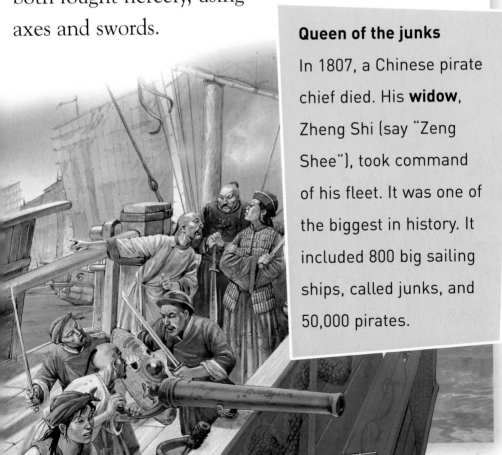

Queen of the junks

In 1807, a Chinese pirate
chief died. His **widow**,
Zheng Shi (say "Zeng
Shee"), took command
of his fleet. It was one of
the biggest in history. It
included 800 big sailing
ships, called junks, and
50,000 pirates.

11

Pirate ships

Pirate ships have always looked a lot like other ships. After all, they were often ordinary ships that the pirates had stolen and given new names. Pirates preferred ships that were fast and able to change direction easily in case they had to make a quick getaway. They also needed ships that were small enough to hide away in **inlets** and bays.

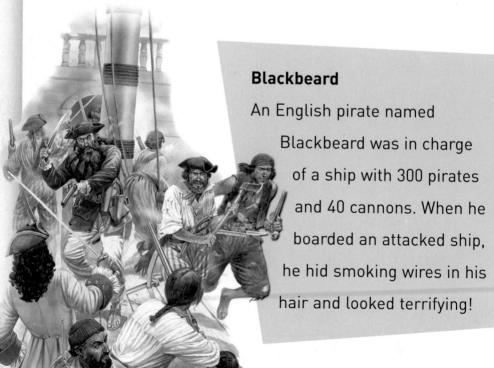

Blackbeard

An English pirate named Blackbeard was in charge of a ship with 300 pirates and 40 cannons. When he boarded an attacked ship, he hid smoking wires in his hair and looked terrifying!

The **Barbary corsairs** were pirates from North Africa in the 1500s. They used fast boats called **galleys**, which had sails and oars. The people they captured were chained and forced to row as galley **slaves**.

In the 1600s, the buccaneers often used long, low sailing canoes. In the 1700s, pirates in North America and the Caribbean preferred speedy sailing ships called **sloops** or **schooners**.

Flags of death

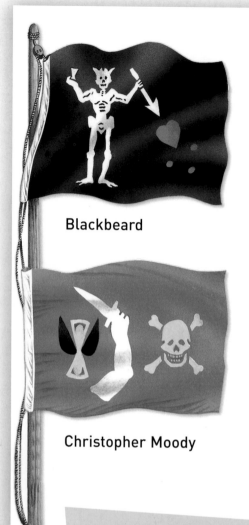

Blackbeard

Christopher Moody

The Barbary corsairs flew red flags on their galleys. Other pirates also chose red, the color of blood, for their ships. The flags meant one thing: expect no mercy! Later, pirate flags were often colored black and red, black and white, or plain black. They were known as **blackjacks** or **Jolly Rogers**.

Tricks and trickery

Sometimes pirates used tricks to take over a ship. They raised the flag of a country to fool their victims as they approached them. Then, at the last moment, they would raise their pirate flag instead.

Calico Jack (John Rackham)

Henry "Long Ben" Avery

Many pirate captains flew their own personal flags. Calico Jack's flag design was a skull with crossed **cutlasses**. An English pirate captain named Henry Avery flew a flag with a skull and crossbones design. Bartholomew Roberts's flag showed him holding hands with a skeleton. This scary Welsh pirate captured over 470 ships!

Bartholomew Roberts

Thomas Tew

15

Life at sea

Pirates had to be good sailors. They had to **navigate**, using the sun or stars to find their way, and read charts. They had to climb the **mast** in the middle of a storm to raise or lower sails. They needed to be able to handle all sorts of weapons, such as pistols, swords, knives, and axes.

Sometimes pirates had to haul their ship up onto a beach to clean the **hull** or repair broken timbers. This was a dangerous time for them. They could be captured by a **navy patrol**.

Sometimes pirates fought each other. In 1697, Captain William Kidd had an argument with his gunner, William Moore. Kidd killed him with a single blow to the head, using a bucket.

Disgusting dishes!
It was hard to keep food fresh during a long voyage. Worms and bugs got into biscuits. And meat had to be very salty to keep it from spoiling.

Crews repaired leaks and mended a broken rudder.

Treasure chests

Pirates wanted treasure that was easy to transport, easy to divide among themselves, and easy to sell. The best treasure was gold or silver coins, metal bars, jewelry, or weapons.

Coin toss!
Gold and silver coins in the Caribbean were called **pieces of eight**, **doubloons**, and **moidores**. A French pirate named Antonio Fuët once ran out of cannonballs, so he loaded his guns with gold coins instead. After that, they called him Captain Moidore.

Some pirate captains liked to steal and wear pieces of fancy clothing. They often wore gold **braid**, lace cuffs, or **plumed** hats.

English pirate Henry "Long Ben" Avery stole one of the biggest treasures of all time. In 1695, he attacked Indian ships in the Red Sea. They belonged to the Indian emperor and were loaded with treasure. The attack was very brutal and violent, but Long Ben made a fortune.

Pirate tales often tell of treasure chests buried on lonely islands or of secret pirate maps. People are *still* searching for buried treasure today!

These pirates buried stolen treasure on an island.

Pirate havens

Pirates needed safe places, called **havens**, to anchor and unload their boats. These havens were usually in remote areas where the pirates lived and sold their **spoils** without being caught. There used to be pirate havens in many parts of the world.

One pirate haven was Port Royal in Jamaica. Buccaneers anchored there beginning in 1655.

Port Royal, Jamaica, in the 1660s

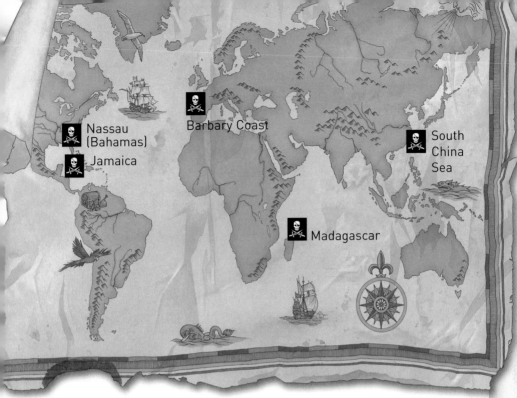

Nassau
(Bahamas)

Barbary Coast

South
China
Sea

Jamaica

Madagascar

The island of Madagascar, off the coast of Africa, was also popular with pirates. One pirate, named Abraham Samuel, was shipwrecked there. He ruled the island as a king from 1697 to 1705!

This map shows popular pirate havens in the 1600s and 1700s.

Ruled by pirates

Between 1614 and 1660, the port of Salé in Morocco, North Africa, was ruled by Barbary corsairs. These pirates went raiding as far away as England, Iceland, and Newfoundland.

Terrible deeds

We can read many exciting stories about pirates. But we should not forget that pirates were criminals. They broke the law and often hurt people. This is true of today's pirates too.

Chinese pirates sometimes nailed their victims to the deck. The pirates of Borneo often chopped off their victims' heads. In the 1600s, a buccaneer named François l'Ollonois used his cutlass to cut out his enemy's heart.

The Barbary corsairs often held their victims as prisoners and would not let them go until someone paid a fee called a **ransom**.

Sometimes pirates left their victims on desert islands, where they could starve to death. This was called marooning. Often pirates just set their prisoners **adrift** at sea in a small boat, with very little food.

These pirates demanded a ransom from a wealthy man they captured.

Pirate hunters

For as long as there have been pirates,
navy patrols have hunted them down
to stop them.

In 1718, the British navy
caught Blackbeard in
North Carolina. He
received 25 wounds by pistol
and cutlass before he fell
down. His head was chopped
off and put on the front
of the ship.

Bartholomew Roberts was hunted
down on the African coast in 1722.
He was badly wounded trying to get away. His
crew buried him at sea before the navy could
take his body away.

British ships attacked the junks of the Chinese pirates.

Sometimes there were big battles with fleets of pirate ships. In 1849, the British navy fought a great battle against Chinese pirates near Hong Kong. Nearly 400 pirates were killed.

Pirates' biggest defeat

In 66 BCE, the Romans went to war with pirates in the Mediterranean Sea. They captured 20,000 of them and killed 10,000 more.

25

Punishment

A few pirates won fame and fortune, but most died in battle, drowned, or ended up as beggars.

Many pirates were brought to trial. If they were found guilty, some pirates had their heads cut off or they were shot. Most often, pirates were hanged in public. Their dead bodies were left hanging in iron cages where all who sailed by could see them.

Dragged to death

William de Marisco attacked ships in the Irish Sea. He was captured in 1242. He was dragged through the streets of London by horses. Then, his body was chopped into four pieces and burned.

A pirate's body was hung in an iron cage as a warning to others.

Clues to the past

Which stories about pirates are true? Which ones are made up? The best way to find out is to look up court records. They name the pirates and the crimes they really did.

Another good way to find out about pirates is to study their shipwrecks. In 1984, the remains of a ship called the *Whydah* were discovered off Cape Cod. The ship belonged to pirate "Black Sam" Bellamy. It was wrecked in a storm in 1717. In the remains, divers found gold bars, coins, cannons, swords, and the ship's bell.

THE
TRYALS
OF
Captain John Rackam,
AND OTHER
PIRATES, *Viz.*

Geroge Fetherston,   Noah Harwood,
Richard Corner,   James Dobbins,
John Davies,   Patrick Carty,
John Howell,   Thomas Earl,
Tho. Bourn, *alias* Brown, John Fenwick, *at* Fenis

Who were all Condemn'd for PIRACY, *at the Town of* St. Jago de
la Vega, *in the Island of* JAMAICA, *on Wednesday and Thursday
the Sixteenth and Seventeenth Days of November* 1720.

AS ALSO, THE

TRYALS *of* Mary Read *and* Anne Bonny,
alias Bonn, *on Monday the* 28th *Day of the
said Month of* November, *at* St. Jago
de la Vega *aforesaid.*

And of several Others, who were also condemn'd for PIRACY.

ALSO,

A True Copy of the Act of Parliament made for the more effectual suppression of Piracy.

Jamaica: Printed by Robert Baldwin, in the Year 1721.

This is a report from the 1721 trials of John Rackham, Anne Bonny, and Mary Read.

Divers show coins they found in the wreck of the *Whydah*.

Timeline

Glossary

adrift floating on the sea

Barbary corsairs pirates from the North African coast who sailed from the 1500s to the 1800s

blackjacks pirate flags of the 1690s and 1700s, such as the skull and crossbones

braid decorative cord, often in silver or gold

buccaneers Caribbean pirates of the 1600s

cargo goods carried by ships

cutlasses deadly slashing swords used by sailors from the 1600s onward

doubloons old Spanish gold coins

galleys wooden ships that use oars as well as sails

havens safe places

hull the frame of a ship

inlets parts of the coast that form narrow bays

Jolly Rogers pirate flags, especially the skull and crossbones

knighted given the title "Sir" by a king or queen

marooned left behind on an island

mast a tall part of a ship to which sails are attached

moidores old gold coins used in Portugal and Brazil

mutineers sailors or soldiers who disobey orders

mutiny a rebellion against a ship's officers or army officers

navigate to find one's way, or to keep a ship on course

navy a country's ships and their crews

patrol a group of sailors or soldiers sent to look out for enemies

pieces of eight old Spanish coins

plumed having a fancy feather or crest

privateer a captain who is given special permission to attack certain ships

ransom a sum of money paid to set a prisoner free

schooners small, fast sailing ships, usually with two masts

seafarers sailors or mariners—people who go to sea

slaves people whose freedom is taken away and who are forced to work for no money

sloops small, fast sailing ships with one mast

spoils money made from crime, or stolen treasure

widow a woman whose husband has died

Index